Captain Corelli's and the Latin trilogy

Music inspired by the novels of Louis de Bernières

Arranged for solo piano by
RICHARD HARRIS

FABER *ff* MUSIC

FOREWORD

One of the curious side-effects of the popularity of *Captain Corelli's Mandolin* is that a lot of people have been inspired to think up projects of their own. Here is one example, which I wish bon voyage on its way from Richard Harris' hands to yours.

As I don't play the piano, I will have to rely on someone else to play them for me, unless I make some transcriptions for classical guitar. On the other hand, I might learn piano after all, and what might that lead to? Private Prokofiev's Pianoforte? Well, maybe I'll let that pass.

Louis de Bernières

CONTENTS

Extracts from *Captain Corelli's Mandolin* (May 1995), *The War of Don Emmanuel's Nether Parts* (August 1997), *The Troublesome Offspring of Cardinal Guzman* (September 1998) and *Señor Vivo and the Coca Lord* (February 1998) by Louis de Bernières, published by Vintage. Used by permission of Pantheon Books and The Random House Group Ltd.

© 2001 by Faber Music Ltd
First published in 2001 by Faber Music Ltd
Bloomsbury House
74–77 Great Russell Street
London WC1B 3DA
Cover illustration by Jeff Fisher
Music processed by Donald Sheppard
Printed in England by Caligraving Ltd
All rights reserved

ISBN10: 0-571-52092-8
EAN13: 978-0-571-52092-3

To buy Faber Music publications or to find out about the full range of titles available
please contact your local music retailer or Faber Music sales enquiries:

Faber Music Limited, Burnt Mill, Elizabeth Way, Harlow, CM20 2HX England
Tel: +44 (0)1279 82 89 82   Fax: +44 (0)1279 82 89 83
sales@fabermusic.com   fabermusicstore.com

How like a woman is a mandolin, how gracious and how lovely.
CAPTAIN CORELLI'S MANDOLIN

Antonia—Captain Corelli's Mandolin

Stephen Warbeck

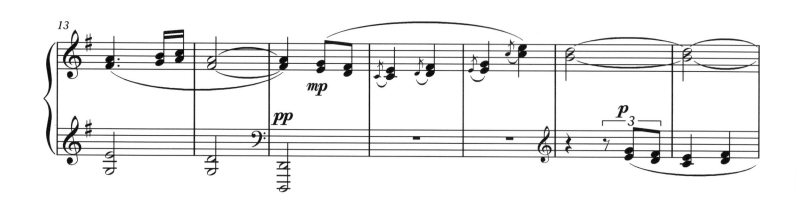

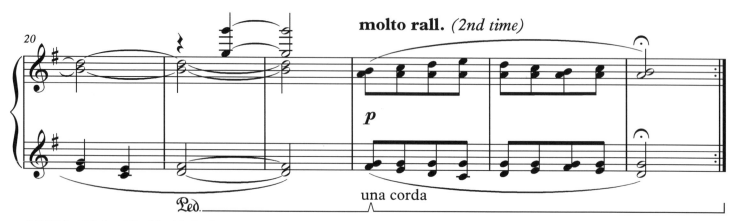

*'We can sing love songs', said Corelli, 'because tonight is a beautiful night …
and we should be thinking about being romantic.'*

CAPTAIN CORELLI'S MANDOLIN

La scala

I La donna è mobile

Giuseppe Verdi (1813–1901)
arr. Richard Harris

One of the tenors of La scala began the 'Humming Chorus' from Madama Butterfly,
and soon others joined in or dropped out, as the catch in their throats permitted.
CAPTAIN CORELLI'S MANDOLIN

II Humming Chorus
from *Madama Butterfly*

Giacomo Puccini (1858–1924)
arr. Richard Harris

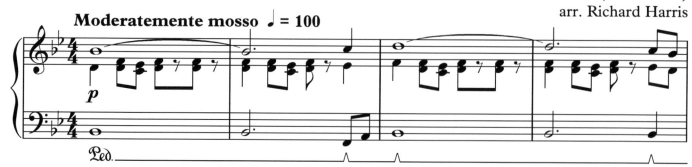

I had a plan to become the best mandolin player in Italy …
I didn't want to be a café player, I wanted to play Hummel and Conforto and Giuliani.
CAPTAIN CORELLI'S MANDOLIN

Grand duo concertant, Op. 85

Mauro Giuliani (1781–1829)
arr. Richard Harris

A posse of the fishermen known as tratoloi *began to open bottles and sing lustily all the songs they had been perfecting for weeks in the tavernas of Panagopoula.*

CAPTAIN CORELLI'S MANDOLIN

Tsamikos et kleftikos

Greek trad.
arr. Richard Harris

I am playing one of Hummel's Concertos for Mandolin. The first forty-five and a half bars
are for the orchestra, allegro moderato e grazioso. You have to imagine the orchestra.

CAPTAIN CORELLI'S MANDOLIN

Andante con variazioni
from *Concerto for Mandolin in G major*

Johann Hummel
(1778–1837)
arr. Richard Harris

He played her sentimental songs from forgotten times.
CAPTAIN CORELLI'S MANDOLIN

Santa Lucia

Teodoro Cottrau (1827–1879)
arr. Richard Harris

It was a march of a proud woman who prosecuted war with hard words and kindnesses.
CAPTAIN CORELLI'S MANDOLIN

Pelagia's March

Richard Harris

[Pelagia] … had never before heard such elaborate virtuosity,
and never before had she found a piece of music to be so full of surprises.

CAPTAIN CORELLI'S MANDOLIN

Polcha variata

for mandolin

Benedetto Persichini (*c.*1880/90–?)
arr. Richard Harris

I think of Pelagia in terms of chords … they ring in each others' aftermath
like soprano and alto in the same key in a Tuscan song.

CAPTAIN CORELLI'S MANDOLIN

For Pelagia

Stephen Warbeck

con Ped.

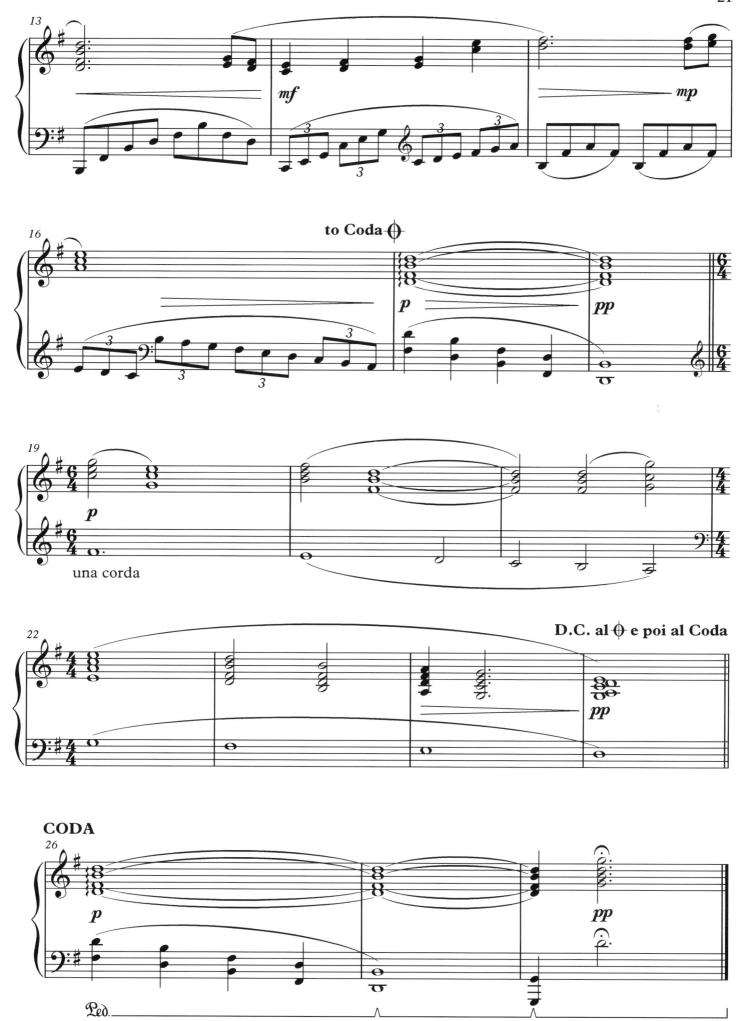

*… everybody was crazy about Bambuco and Vallenato, two types of dance music
characterised by a fascinating complexity of syncopation.*

THE WAR OF DON EMMANUEL'S NETHER PARTS

Fiesta

Richard Harris

We have a certain cure here in our hands ... we call it La danza del fuego.

SEÑOR VIVO AND THE COCA LORD

Firedance

Richard Harris

It was a place where one could find spectacular revelry and good humour.

THE TROUBLESOME OFFSPRING OF CARDINAL GUZMAN

Cielito Lindo

Mexican trad.
arr. Richard Harris

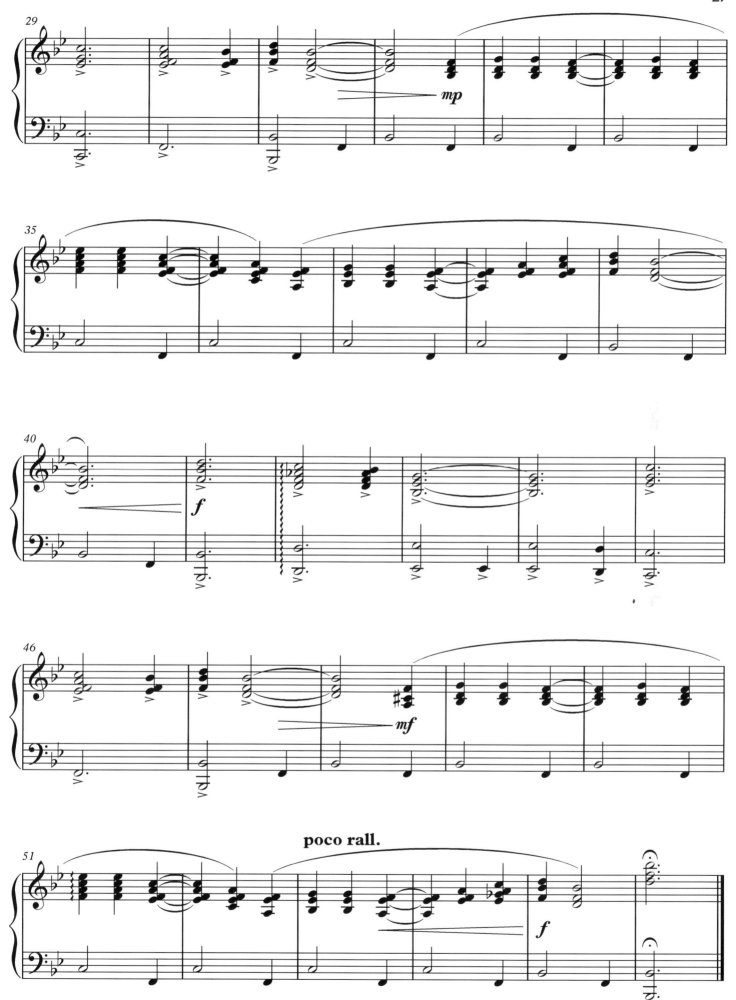

It was being played by a small group of musicians …
it moved the whole congregation to tears, myself not excepted.
THE TROUBLESOME OFFSPRING OF CARDINAL GUZMAN

Requiem of Angels

Richard Harris

Stephen Warbeck

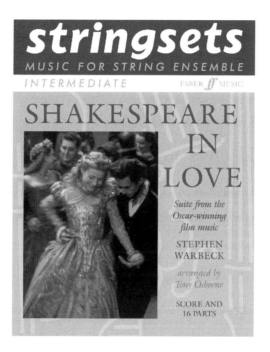

Stephen Warbeck's Oscar-winning music for the hit film *Shakespeare in Love* has here been skilfully arranged by Tony Osborne into a four-movement suite for intermediate string ensemble.

The suite perfectly encapsulates all the passion, romance and wit of this delightful love story, which traces the footsteps of the young Shakespeare. With an exciting opening, sighing love-themes and two rhythmic dances, which capture the atmosphere of the vibrant Elizabethan court, this contrasted suite will stir the players' and audiences' imagination and allow it to take flight.

To buy Faber Music publications or to find out about the full range of titles available please contact your local music retailer or Faber Music sales enquiries:

Faber Music Ltd, Burnt Mill, Elizabeth Way, Harlow CM20 2HX
Tel: +44 (0) 1279 82 89 82   Fax: +44 (0) 1279 82 89 83
sales@fabermusic.com   fabermusicstore.com

Albums from Faber Music

PIANO

Captain Corelli's Mandolin *Richard Harris*

ISBN 0-571-52092-8

Children's Album *arranged by Daniel Scott*

ISBN 0-571-51103-1

The Essential Showtunes Collection *arranged by Richard Harris*

ISBN 0-571-52782-5

The Essential Film Collection *arranged by Richard Harris*

ISBN 0-571-52781-7

Great Film and TV Themes *Carl Davis*

ISBN 0-571-51740-4

Jane Austen's World *arranged by Richard Harris*

ISBN 0-571-51793-5

Shakespeare's World *arranged by Richard Harris*

ISBN 0-571-51907-5

Cult Classics *Richard Harris*

ISBN 0-571-52096-0

FABER *ff* MUSIC

To buy Faber Music publications or to find out about the full range of titles available
please contact your local music retailer or Faber Music sales enquiries:

Faber Music Ltd, Burnt Mill, Elizabeth Way, Harlow CM20 2HX
Tel: +44 (0) 1279 82 89 82   Fax: +44 (0) 1279 82 89 83
sales@fabermusic.com   fabermusicstore.com